999

D0070356

# LET'S VISIT THE GAMBIA

# Let's visit
# THE GAMBIA

FRANCES WILKINS

First published 1985
© Frances Wilkins 1985
All rights reserved. No part of this publication may be reproduced, stored in a retrieval system, or transmitted, in any form or by any means, electronic, mechanical, photocopying, recording or otherwise, without the prior permission of Burke Publishing Company Limited.

## ACKNOWLEDGEMENTS

The author and publishers are grateful to the following organizations and individuals for permission to reproduce copyright photographs in this book:

Camerapix Hutchison Photo Library Ltd., Colorpix Photo Library Ltd., The Mansell Collection Ltd.

**CIP data**
Wilkins, Frances
  Let's visit The Gambia
  1.  Gambia  –  Social life and customs  –  Juvenile literature
  I.  Title
  966'.5103      DT509.8

ISBN 0 222 01129 7

Burke Publishing Company Limited
Pegasus House, 116-120 Golden Lane, London EC1Y 0TL, England.
Burke Publishing (Canada) Limited
*Registered Office:* 20 Queen Street West, Suite 3000, Box 30, Toronto, Canada M5H 1V5.
Burke Publishing Company Inc.
*Registered Office:* 333 State Street, PO Box 1740, Bridgeport, Connecticut 06601, U.S.A.
Filmset in Baskerville by Graphiti (Hull) Ltd., Hull, England.
Colour reproduction by Swift Graphics (UK) Ltd., Southampton, England.
Printed in Singapore by Tien Wah Press (Pte.) Ltd.

# Contents

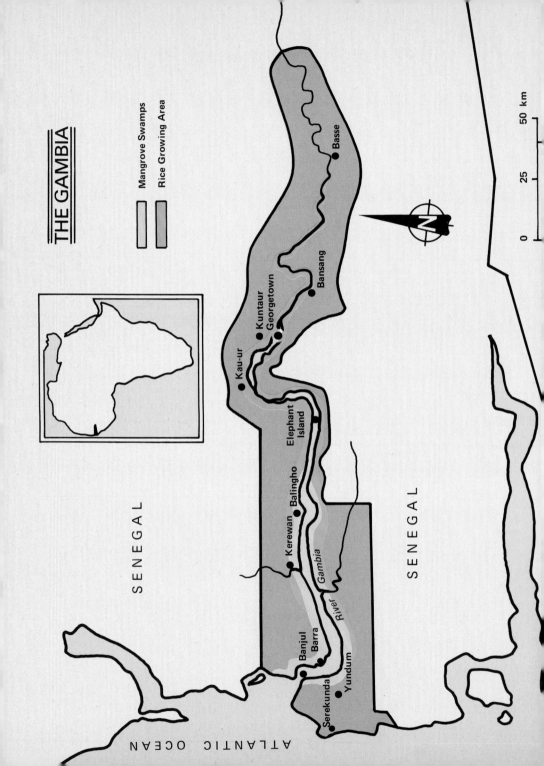

THE GAMBIA

Mangrove Swamps

Rice Growing Area

SENEGAL

SENEGAL

ATLANTIC OCEAN

Banjul
Barra
Serekunda
Yundum
Kerewan
Balingho
Elephant Island
Kau-ur
Kuntaur
Georgetown
Bansang
Basse

Gambia River

N

0    25    50 km

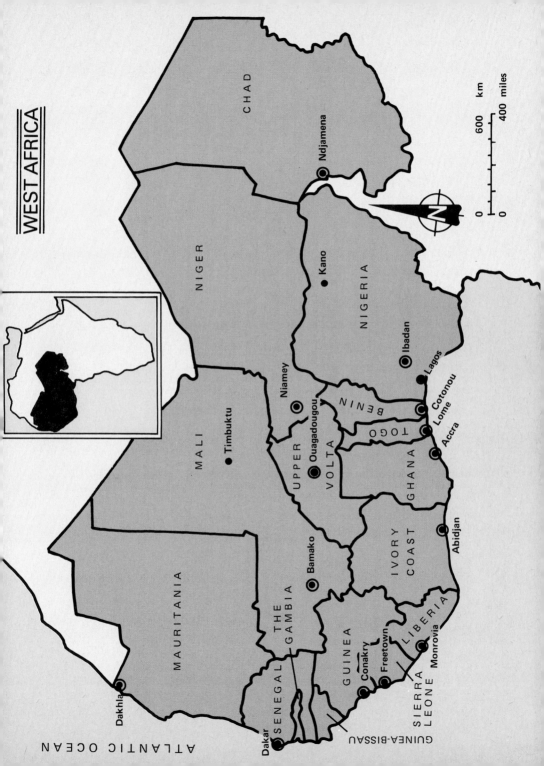

WEST AFRICA

ATLANTIC OCEAN

CHAD

NIGER

MALI

MAURITANIA

NIGERIA

BENIN

TOGO

GHANA

IVORY COAST

UPPER VOLTA

THE GAMBIA

SENEGAL

GUINEA

SIERRA LEONE

LIBERIA

GUINEA-BISSAU

Ndjamena

Kano

Ibadan

Lagos

Cotonou

Lome

Accra

Abidjan

Monrovia

Freetown

Conakry

Bamako

Ouagadougou

Niamey

Timbuktu

Dakar

Dakhla

0    600    km

0    400 miles

# The Land and the People

The Gambia is a long narrow strip of land—about 320 kilometres (200 miles) east to west, and for most of its length only about 24 kilometres (16 miles) north to south. It is on the west coast of Africa and, apart from the short stretch of the country facing the Atlantic, is entirely surrounded by Senegal.

Although The Gambia is so small, it is crossed by a huge river. This is the River Gambia which flows from east to west, dividing the country into two. The river is navigable by ocean-going vessels for about half its length in The Gambia; and small boats, such as launches and canoes, can even reach those riverbank settlements and villages which lie furthest inland.

Geographically, The Gambia can be divided into three regions. First, there is the coastal area to the south of the river, including a number of islands. This is the most low-lying part of the country, and it is generally very sandy. Because of this, it is of little agricultural use, apart from growing palm trees of various types.

**A ship in Banjul port at the mouth of the River Gambia. Even large ocean-going vessels such as this can sail as far as half-way up the river, whatever the state of the tide**

The next region is formed by the area on either side of the River Gambia. For about half its length this region is flooded with sea water once a year. As a result, it is covered with mangrove forests. However, the rest of the area is flooded by fresh water. This land becomes extremely fertile once the water has gone down, and it is used mainly for growing rice.

The third region is formed by the savannah (or grasslands) bordering on Senegal. This is the highest part of the country, although it never reaches more than 200 metres (650 feet) above sea level. The grasslands are not as fertile as the rice-growing area, because they are far drier, but they are ideal for growing groundnuts—the country's most important crop.

The climate of The Gambia is reasonably healthy. The temperature seldom rises above 36° Centigrade (97°

9

Fahrenheit), and rarely falls below 10° Centigrade (50° Fahrenheit). The total annual rainfall is not more than 1,500 millimetres (60 inches), and it virtually all falls during the short rainy season from June to October. Europeans find the rainy season rather trying. The heat and the high humidity make people feel sticky and uncomfortable. But most people find the long, dry season quite pleasant, especially on the coast, where the heat is usually tempered by cool breezes from the sea.

Being relatively fertile, The Gambia has attracted settlers from

**Coconut palms in the sandy soil of the coastal area**

**Part of the rice-growing area alongside the River Gambia**

many other parts of West Africa. As a result, the population today is made up of a number of different ethnic groups. Out of a total population of about 700,000 over forty per cent are Mandingo, while the rest are mostly Fula, Wolof and Jola. There are also a certain number of Senegalese.

Each different ethnic group in The Gambia has its own language, and news and other items are regularly broadcast in five different tongues. For all government purposes, however, the official language is English—but outside Banjul, the capital, this is hardly spoken or understood at all.

About seventy per cent of the people in The Gambia are Muslims. About five per cent are Christians—approximately half of these are Roman Catholics, while the others are either Anglicans or Methodists. There are also groups of Gambians,

11

particularly in the more remote country districts, who cling to their old primitive belief in animism. This means that they believe that everything, from the sun to the river and from the moon to the crops, has a spirit of its own. Their worship usually consists of all kinds of magic incantations, to try to persuade the good spirits to help them and the evil spirits to leave them alone. Officially, only twenty-five per cent of the population are animists, but the actual figure is probably considerably higher.

As the population of The Gambia is so small, there are no very large cities. The largest is the capital, Banjul (formerly called Bathurst), which has approximately 80,000 inhabitants. It is situated on a small island at the mouth of the River Gambia, and is the country's most important port, with about three hundred ships calling in every year. The next largest town is Serekunda, with a population of about 25,000. It is only a short distance from Banjul and not very far from the coast. Apart from these two places, there are only seven towns in The Gambia with more than 3,000 inhabitants. The rest of the country's population live either in villages or in small, remote hamlets.

The Gambia's economy is based almost entirely on the exporting of groundnuts. No other country in Africa is so dependent on one single crop. This means that when there is a bad groundnut harvest, as occurred in 1980-81, the country can easily find itself on the brink of financial disaster.

The Gambians themselves cannot cope with all the work involved in growing the groundnuts. So about 20,000 seasonal workers, mostly from Senegal, arrive to help them every year.

12

**A groundnut buying-station. Farmers deliver their crops to stations such as this, where the government's marketing board fixes the season's prices and distributes the groundnuts for processing**

No foreign worker is ever directly employed by a Gambian farmer, however. The foreigner merely rents a small piece of land from the farmer and gives him a share of the profit in return.

After agriculture, the major industry in The Gambia is tourism. There are more than a dozen modern hotels lining the sea-front west of Banjul, and these accommodate more than twenty thousand visitors a year. Apart from sun-bathing and swimming, the main attraction is bird-watching. More than four hundred different species of birds, including kingfishers, cuckoos, swallows, herons, doves, grass warblers and hawks, have been seen in The Gambia in recent years.

**Part of The Gambia's sandy coastline—a major attraction for the thousands of tourists who visit The Gambia each year**

The Gambia has been an independent country only since February, 1965, and it has been a republic (within the Commonwealth of Nations) only since April, 1970.

The head of state of The Gambia is the President—at present Sir Dawda Jawara. He is elected by popular vote and serves for a term of five years. The country is governed by a House of Representatives, with forty-nine members. Of these, thirty-five are chosen by popular vote and sit for five years, while the rest are nominated by various individuals and groups of people. The leader of the government (roughly equivalent to a prime

14

minister) is the Vice-President, and he is assisted by a cabinet which currently consists of twelve members.

Most of the Gambians are extremely loyal and proud of their country. They have a national anthem, *Na Gambia Banko Kamma* ("For The Gambia, Our Homeland"). They also have a national flag which always flies from the government buildings. The flag has three broad horizontal bands—red, blue and green—separated from each other by narrow bands of white.

Finally, why is the country called The Gambia? The story is that one of the early European explorers asked a native the name of the country, and the answer was "Kambi". In fact, this was the native's own name, but by the time people realized this the name had stuck!

## Early Times

Very little is known about the early history of The Gambia. No one knows, for example, when people first decided to settle in this area, or what they were like. But primitive stone circles and a few primitive tools and weapons prove that people were certainly living on both banks of the River Gambia by about A.D. 1000.

The first reliable records of this area date from the early thirteenth century. This was when traders from a tribe called the Mandingo began to be seen along the banks of the River Gambia. It was no doubt these traders who spread the news that the river-banks were relatively fertile in some places; and it was this which made various other people begin to think of settling there.

The first hostile invaders arrived in about A.D. 1235. They were the Kangaba (closely related to the Mandingo) who, under King Sundiata, eventually conquered a large part of West Africa. Sundiata established his capital at a new city which he

16

called Mali, and from then on all the land he ruled came to be known as the Mali Empire.

The Mali Empire was at its height under a king named Mansa Musa. He was a very able ruler, who reigned from about 1312 until about 1337. Under Mansa Musa the Mali Empire included not only the country which is now The Gambia, but also present-day Mali, Senegal and Guinea, as well as parts of Mauritania, Niger and Upper Volta.

Many cities in the Mali Empire were important centres of the caravan trade. Merchants regularly set out from there to trade with people on the far side of the Sahara Desert. At the same time, many people in the Mali Empire were successful farmers, growing rice and cotton (among other things). Yet others were herdsmen, looking after various types of cattle and sheep.

Culture and learning also flourished in the Mali Empire. Timbuktu, in present-day Mali, was a famous centre of study, particularly for law. Timbuktu was also renowned as a place for Islamic studies, as most of the ruling class in the Mali Empire were Muslims—although the ordinary country people generally continued to worship their old pagan gods.

The control of such a vast empire obviously needed considerable skill. But the rulers who succeeded Mansa Musa had none of his outstanding ability and drive. As a result, from about 1400 onwards a people called the Songhoi, among others, began to conquer the more outlying parts of the Mali Empire. By about 1500 they had taken possession of almost all of it.

**A mosque in Timbuktu, in present-day Mali. At the time of the Mali Empire, Timbuktu was renowned as a centre for Islamic studies**

Unfortunately, very little is known about any of these new invaders. Some people think that the Songhoi came from present-day Sudan, but this has never been conclusively proved. It is generally agreed, however, that these invaders finally lost control of the area in about 1591, and that the land on both sides of the River Gambia later fell into the hands of various small, semi-nomadic tribes.

Meanwhile, in about 1455, the first Europeans had arrived in West Africa. They were Portuguese, and they were looking for anything they could find to take home and sell at a profit. They were particularly keen to find slaves, as there was always

18

a demand for strong young labourers in those days—especially when the New World was discovered, with its vast new possibilities for plantations.

It was not easy for the Portuguese to gain a foothold in West Africa, however. The heavy breakers made it extremely difficult for the flimsy boats of that period even to approach the sea-shore. It was also almost impossible for them to sail up most of the West African rivers, because of all the waterfalls and rapids, caused by the high rocky areas not far inland. Nevertheless, a few forts were finally established, as well as a small number of coastal settlements. These acted as both trading stations and supply points for ships going on to southern Africa and south-east Asia. But the Portuguese made little attempt to penetrate further inland, as the mangrove swamps and the dense forests, combined with the tropical heat, formed an almost impenetrable barrier.

For two hundred years the situation remained much the same. The Portuguese were joined by traders from many other European countries, particularly Spain, France and Britain. But very few permanent settlements were established—mainly because the land was too inhospitable, but also because most of the people who did try to settle there soon contracted and died of some tropical disease, such as malaria or yellow fever.

Then, in 1661, a group of English traders were given a charter by their government which gave them the right to form a company called ''The Royal Adventurers Trading to Africa''. They founded a small settlement at a place which they called

Fort James, in what is now The Gambia, and they were soon doing a thriving trade, particularly in slaves.

This gave the British their first foothold in The Gambia. After that, their influence gradually spread until they controlled almost all the area which today makes up the country. Then, in 1765, the British managed to acquire Senegal from the French, and the Crown Colony of Senegambia was formed, with its capital at Saint-Louis at the mouth of the River Senegal.

This arrangement lasted for only a few years, however. In 1783 Senegal was handed back to the French, and Senegambia ceased to exist. The Gambia itself continued to be a British possession and was never seriously affected by the rivalry among the various European powers who wanted to gain all the land they possibly could in West Africa.

**Cannon in Banjul, The Gambia's capital, dating from the time of British colonial rule**

Unfortunately, the British were never particularly popular in The Gambia. This was mainly because the Gambians (like the other West Africans) could never forget that the white men had originally come to their country to make them slaves. But the British undoubtedly brought a much better way of life to The Gambia, by introducing new crops and new farming methods, and by greatly improving the standard of the roads and the sanitation.

Even as late as the nineteen-thirties, however, the whole of West Africa was still known as "the white man's grave". This was because so many white settlers died within two or three years of arriving there. But the diseases that killed them, such as malaria, can all be avoided with modern pills and injections; and, although they are still rife in The Gambia, today's European holiday-makers probably never give them a thought.

All the dates in this chapter refer, of course, to the Western (or Christian) calendar. But the Gambians themselves, being Muslims, officially date events in the Islamic manner. The first day of their era is the day Muhammad left Mecca for Medina, which by Western reckoning was July 16th, A.D. 622. This means that the Western year 2000 is the Muslim year 1378.

# The Slave Trade

The most unhappy period in West Africa's history began in the late fifteenth century. This was when the Portuguese started going to what is now The Gambia and other neighbouring countries to try to find slaves. The Portuguese would wait in hiding until the Africans, male or female, came out of the bush to wash on the river-bank or on the seashore. Then they would seize them and force them into the holds of their ships.

It was not long, however, before the Africans learned to keep out of sight. So the Portuguese began buying slaves from any native ruler who had managed to take prisoners from some other local tribe. The traders usually gave the rulers weapons, such as spears and daggers, or some tools; and sometimes they gave them some kind of alcoholic drink or tobacco.

Then the discovery of America caused a sudden expansion in the slave trade. At first, the Spaniards who had settled in the New World forced the American Indians to work in their mines or on their plantations. But the Spaniards soon found

**This prison was used by French, English and Dutch traders to house slaves awaiting shipment to the Americas**

that there were not enough native workers to meet their requirements, and they began to look around for some other source of labour.

This was the very opportunity for which the slave-traders had been waiting. From about 1620 onwards, the Portuguese and the Spanish traders could not ship their African slaves across the Atlantic fast enough. Prosperous colonists everywhere in America and the West Indies were crying out for cheap labour, particularly in the cotton-fields and on the sugar plantations;

23

and men, women and children were all equally suitable as workers.

The English quickly joined the Portuguese and the Spaniards in the slave trade. In 1771, as many as fifty-eight slave ships left London, and no fewer than 107 left Liverpool. Even the town of Bristol (which was comparatively small in those days) sent twenty-three ships across the Atlantic with slaves; and the slave trade was, in fact, the foundation of the city's later prosperity.

The conditions under which the slaves were taken to the New World were almost indescribable. First, the slaves were chained hand and foot, and branded with the trader's mark, like cattle.

**An eighteenth-century print showing slaves from West Africa working on a sugar plantation in the New World**

**The landing-post for the village of Juffure, made famous by Alex Haley
in his book _Roots_ as the village from which his ancestors were taken
as slaves**

Then they were herded into the holds of the merchants' ships
where, with no sanitation and very little ventilation, many of
them died long before the terrible voyage was over. When they
arrived at their destination, conditions were usually little better.
The slaves were crowded into comfortless compounds or pens
while they were waiting to be sold. Then, husbands separated
from their wives, and children from their parents, they were
sold and taken away to the cotton-fields or to the sugar
plantations.

Almost from the outset, there were three stages in the slave
trade. First, ships left Europe with cheap goods to barter for
slaves in West Africa. Then the slaves were shipped across the

25

Atlantic to America or the West Indies. There, in exchange for slaves, the ships took on board local produce, such as sugar, tobacco, coffee or cotton, and headed back across the Atlantic to Europe. This became known as the "Slave Triangle".

The slave-traders certainly made enormous profits in the early years. But gradually it became more difficult for them to make money. The compounds where the slaves were kept while awaiting shipment had to be guarded, in case the slaves tried to escape; and the ships that took the slaves overseas had to be maintained and armed against pirates. In addition, as soon as more mechanized methods of work were invented, the demand for slaves dropped. Machines were more reliable, had a greater output and cost less. And there were eventually so many slave-trading nations, notably France, Holland and Spain, as well as Britain, that each country had to undercut the others, and profits fell considerably.

Towards the end of the eighteenth century, the story of the terrible sufferings of the slaves somehow began to find its way back to Britain. Many people, especially those with strong religious beliefs, began to denounce the slave trade, believing that everyone was born with a God-given right to be free.

Eventually there was one small incident that brought the public outcry to its peak. A slave tried to escape from his American master while they were on a visit to Britain. As a result, slavery was declared illegal in England in 1807, and it was only a very short time before all the other European countries followed suit.

A cartoon, ironically entitled "Christian Practices", first published in 1792. At this time Europeans were just starting to become aware of how cruelly and unjustly slaves were treated

Curiously enough, the slave trade actually increased after it was forbidden. Traders seemed to think that there would be a shortage of slaves, and that they could get a good price for them. In fact, for a time the Royal Navy was intercepting one hundred or more slave ships a year—most of them Portuguese, which were hoping to take the slaves to either Cuba or Brazil.

Once the slaves had been freed by the Navy they were taken to resettlement centres. There was one of these in The Gambia, and another in Sierra Leone. They usually stayed there for three months, employed in various government projects, such as road-building, and then they were given a small piece of land and set free.

Eventually, the risks involved in trying to trade in slaves became just too great. It also became apparent that even in South America there was no market for slaves any more. However, the story was by no means over for the West Africans themselves—bitter feuds continued for years between the tribes who had tried to sell each other into slavery and, as one missionary in The Gambia had sadly predicted, the enmity lasted for generations.

Unfortunately, the ending of the slave trade did not bring the West Africans any true freedom. Although they were allowed to stay in their own countries, they were often treated little better than slaves. Possibly the Gambians, being under British rule, were in a slightly happier position; but the difference between one West African country and another was at best only very slight. The white settlers seemed unable to believe that the West Africans were their equals in any way. They produced what they claimed was conclusive proof that the West Africans all had a very low intelligence. Only in much later years, owing to international pressure exerted by such organizations as the League of Nations, were steps finally taken to put a ban on conditions which, if they were not actually slavery, certainly came very close to it.

## Islam

There have been Muslims in The Gambia from the time of the Mali Empire. At first they were mostly the members of the ruling class, but gradually more and more people began to accept the new religion. Today, nearly three-quarters of the population of The Gambia are Muslims. This means that they belong to the religion called Islam, which was founded by a man named Muhammad.

Muhammad was born in Mecca, in present-day Saudi Arabia, in about A.D. 570. His parents were pagans, and believed in countless unseen spirits, known as djinns. But one night Muhammad had a vision, in which an angel spoke to him. The angel told him that there was only one true God, Allah, and that Allah had chosen Muhammad to be his prophet.

Muhammad was deeply moved by this divine revelation. He began urging everyone to give up the old pagan beliefs, and to believe in the one all-powerful creator. But most of the people of Mecca thought that Muhammad was either a liar or a madman, and by the year A.D. 622 they had become so angry with him that they were plotting to kill him.

When Muhammad heard of the plots, he fled from Mecca and went to Medina. This was a town about 400 kilometres (250 miles) to the north, where he already had a number of followers. To his delight, the people of Medina received him with great enthusiasm, and were so impressed with his teaching that they even asked him to become the ruler of their city.

Muhammad then decided to spread his new religion by force of arms. He told his followers that every drop of blood they spilt in fighting for the Islamic religion was equivalent to two months spent in prayer. Finally, in A.D. 630, Muhammad returned to Mecca as a conqueror; and within a few years he had become the spiritual leader of most of the people of the Middle East and North Africa.

The meaning of the word Islam is ''utter submission to God''. Whatever happens to them, good or bad, Muslims always accept it as being the will of Allah. It is sometimes said that this is the reason why Muslims are so slow to improve their way of life, as they feel it is useless to make plans when it is Allah who will decide the course of events.

The Muslim equivalent of the Bible is the *Quran* (Koran). This is a collection of the sayings of Muhammad, which Muslims believe were inspired directly by God. The sayings were collected together by some of Muhammad's friends about a year after his death in A.D. 632, and they give Muslims instructions which cover almost every aspect of their day-to-day lives.

**A mosque in a small Gambian village**

Islam differs from most religions in having no specially trained ministers. The *khatib,* who preaches to the people, and the *imam*, who leads the prayers, are just ordinary Muslims. They are chosen for their piety and learning, but most of them spend only a few hours a week on their religious duties, and usually do some other kind of work the rest of the time.

Muslim places of worship are known as mosques. They usually have a dome, and a slender tower called a minaret, with a crescent on top. Until quite recently, a man called a *muezzin* used to climb to the top of the minaret and shout, ''Allah is great! There is no god but Allah!'' when it was time for prayers. Nowadays, however, the voice of the *muezzin* is usually recorded, and is just relayed from the minaret.

Before entering a mosque Muslims always take off their shoes,

31

or cover them with canvas slippers. This is done partly out of reverence, and partly to keep the dust of the streets out of the mosques. Muslims are also expected to wash their face, hands and feet before they enter, and in the courtyard of most mosques there is a fountain, or a tank of clean water, where this can be done.

To Christians, the interior of a mosque often seems empty and uninteresting. Usually, the only furniture is an elaborately carved pulpit with steps leading up from the front. There are no seats or benches, but each person kneels on a small mat or rug, and touches the ground with his forehead over and over again as he prays. Christians also notice the absence of pictures and statues. These are never seen in a mosque, or anywhere else in the Muslim world for that matter. Muslims believe that it is wrong to try to copy living things, and this is why all the decoration in Muslim countries consists of geometrical designs and patterns of various kinds.

To the Muslims, the most important part of a mosque is the *mihrab*. This is a tall, arched recess in one of the walls, usually close to the pulpit. When Muslims pray they always look towards the *mihrab*, and then they know they are looking towards Mecca. It is one of the commandments of their religion that they must always face Muhammad's birth-place when they pray.

The Muslims' holy day, equivalent to the Christian Sunday, is Friday. Most of the shops and businesses close on a Friday, so that the men can go to the mosques. In some places women also attend. However, women are not allowed to join in the

32

public worship, and must sit either on a balcony or in a special area partitioned off from the main part of the mosque.

Five times a day, when they hear the *muezzin*'s call, Muslims are supposed to face Mecca and pray—at dawn, at midday, in the afternoon, at sunset and after dark. They sometimes go to the mosque to say these prayers, but it is not uncommon to see them unrolling their prayer-mats at home or at work, or even by the side of the road.

One month every year is known to the Muslims as Ramadan. This does not occur at the same time each year, however, as the Muslim calendar is based on the phases of the moon. During

**A shaded corner, reserved for Muslim prayers, near the port in Banjul**

**A Christian church in Banjul**

Ramadan, Muslims may neither eat nor drink while it is daylight, as this is a time—rather like Lent in the Christian calendar—when people try to purify their lives and draw closer to God.

Today, seventy per cent of Gambians are Muslims. However, as we have already seen, there are also large numbers of both Christians and animists in The Gambia. And there are many people who believe in both Islam and animism. This is shown by so-called Muslims who, like the animists, wear "jujus" (charms) round their necks, arms and ankles to ward off evil spirits. Many Muslims also make long treks along with the

34

animists to sacred baobab trees and other supposedly holy places, to pray for such things as recovery from illness, or a child for a childless couple.

Despite the fact that Islam has been the predominant religion in The Gambia for centuries, there are comparatively few mosques or other outward signs of the faith to be seen, except in Banjul. In fact, there can be little doubt that the Muslim teachings are not followed as strictly in The Gambia as they are in the Arab countries where the religion originated. This is particularly true of the more remote rural districts.

## The Gambians

The population of The Gambia is increasing rapidly. According to the 1973 census there were less than half a million prople— although even this was many more than had been estimated. But by 1984 the population was 660,000, and it is estimated that by 1989 the figure will be three-quarters of a million. None of these figures includes the people from Senegal, who regularly visit The Gambia to help with farmwork. There are usually about twenty thousand of these seasonal workers, although the figure varies from year to year. Most of the Senegalese agricultural workers are very young, sometimes only aged 15 to 16, and few of them are over 30 years of age.

From early times, The Gambia has been populated by a mixture of ethnic groups. As the banks of the River Gambia are extremely fertile, they have always attracted quite a number of settlers. As a result, there are five major ethnic groups of black Africans in The Gambia, as well as smaller groups of Senegalese and other West African people.

36

By far the largest single group are the Mandingo (sometimes known as the Malinke). They represent about forty-two per cent of the population, and are found in virtually every part of the country. They are tall, broad-shouldered people, who are very fond of music, and mostly make their living as traders or groundnut farmers.

The next largest group are a nomadic people known as the Fula. These probably represent about twelve per cent of the population, although it is difficult to be precise. Most of the Fula live in the eastern part of The Gambia, and raise cattle, moving from place to place with their herds in search of new grazing grounds.

About ten per cent of The Gambia's population are Wolof. Some of these are farmers who live near the northern borders of the country. But large numbers of them also live in the capital, Banjul, where in fact they make up the majority of the population. The Wolof are well-known as charming, friendly people. It is also the Wolof women who probably correspond most closely with the average white person's idea of a West African. They usually dress elegantly in brightly coloured turbans, and high-waisted, full-skirted dresses, with lots of gold ornaments and jewellery, and they always seem ready to enjoy themselves with music and dancing.

The Jola make up another five per cent of The Gambia's population. Most anthropologists believe that the Jola were the original inhabitants of the land beside the River Gambia, even before the Mandingo arrived. At any rate, they were certainly

**A Mandingo father and son. The Mandingo represent about forty-two per cent of The Gambia's population**

bitter enemies of the Mandingo for many centuries; and even today past feuds and hatreds have not entirely disappeared. The Jola live south of the River Gambia, near the coast. They are mostly hard-working farmers, who live in small villages surrounded by earthen walls. They grow rice and millet for food, and they nearly all follow the old animist religion which was practised by their ancestors hundreds of years ago.

The fifth main ethnic group in The Gambia is the Serahuli. They also make up about five per cent of the population, and they live in the eastern part of The Gambia. They are nearly all engaged in agriculture, but in their part of the country the

38

soil is poor, and farming tends to be extremely laborious and difficult. It is for this reason that the Serahuli call on the Senegalese to come and help them every year. The Senegalese usually come twice—once when the seeds are being sown and again at harvest time. In return for their work, the Senegalese receive an agreed share of the crop, and are also allowed to raise crops on a small piece of land for themselves.

All the various ethnic groups in The Gambia have their own chiefs and elders. But many of these chiefs are beginning to lose their authority as new forms of national and local government are introduced. This may well be a good thing, as many problems have been caused in the past by bitter feuds between

A colourful scene in Banjul market, showing people from different ethnic groups

tribes who are more interested in their own particular needs than in the needs of the country in general.

The density of the population in The Gambia is quite high compared with most other African countries. In fact, there are on average about 60 people per square kilometre (150 people per square mile) of dry land. The population is not distributed evenly, however, as far more people live on the sandstone uplands than on either bank of the river or near the coast. The reason for this is that the uplands are by far the healthiest part of the country. They are well-drained and never become flooded or swampy. On the other hand, the land along the river and by the coast is constantly liable to floods, and the climate tends to be humid and unpleasant.

The only parts of the river-bank where there are a few villages are the middle and upper stretches. In those places there is less danger of flooding and the climate is healthier. There are also a number of villages built between this river-bank area and the inland uplands, where the soil is relatively fertile by the standards of The Gambia.

Unlike most other countries, The Gambia has never had a great drift of people from the country into the towns. Even today about eighty per cent of Gambians still live in the rural areas. Apart from Banjul, which attracts a steady flow of newcomers, most of the towns are only increasing in size at approximately the same rate as the overall growth of the population.

# The River Gambia

The River Gambia is 1,120 kilometres (700 miles) long. It is one of the finest waterways in Africa, and the whole life of The Gambia centres around it. It rises in the Republic of Guinea, flows through Senegal, and eventually reaches The Gambia about 640 kilometres (400 miles) from its source.

When the river enters The Gambia from Senegal, its meanders are what are known as incised. This means that the bends in the river are all much below the level of the land on either side. Later, however, after it has passed McCarthy Island, the valley broadens out, and swamps known as the *banto faros* begin to appear on either side.

At this point, the River Gambia is about 1.6 kilometres (one mile) in width. This is far wider than any European river so far from its mouth. It also appears to be even wider than it is, because of the *banto faros*, which become more extensive as the river nears the sea.

Long before Elephant Island the *banto faros* are even wider

41

than the river itself. In fact, there is often no firm ground for one or even two kilometres (in some places as much as a mile) from the edge of the river. Normally the first firm ground is the sharp slopes that lead to the uplands. (The uplands form the sandstone plateau which borders the river on either side for a great part of its length.) In some places, however, there is an isolated hill in the *banto faros*. These hills are the remnants of ancient uplands which still exist because they are made of solid rock. They are usually extremely steep, but they can be useful to farmers for growing crops, as they are generally covered with a layer of fine soil, very well-drained and fertile.

Below Elephant Island the river is still bordered by the *banto faros*. But by this time it has become an estuary, and is salt for at least part of the year. The actual limit of the salt water varies—it creeps up almost as far as Kau-ur in the dry season

**A ferry approaching McCarthy Island**

People boarding a boat at a landing-stage on the River Gambia. The whole life of The Gambia centres around the river

but, when the rains come, the rush of water downwards pushes it much closer to the sea.

The *banto faros* continue along both sides of the river as it approaches its mouth. But there are also mangrove swamps all along the banks by this time, so the river looks quite different. Finally the river broadens out, and is joined by a tributary on either side, before it makes its final bend northwards towards Banjul, and flows into the Atlantic Ocean.

**Mangrove swamps, which lie alongside the river as it approaches the sea but before it broadens out**

Just before it reaches Banjul, the river is 11 kilometres (7 miles wide). Then it narrows for a short distance to about 5 kilometres (3 miles) between Banjul and Barra. But at its mouth, at Cape St. Mary, it is over 19 kilometres (12 miles) wide; and although there is a sandbar there is always a channel, at least 8 metres (26 feet) deep, along which ships can sail.

The River Gambia is, in fact, one of the most navigable of all African rivers. It can always be entered by ocean-going vessels, whatever the state of the tide. Ships up to 3,000 tonnes can sail all the way from Banjul to Kau-ur, a distance of 200 kilometres (120 miles); and smaller vessels can even reach the frontier with Senegal, in the far east of the country.

Until recently, even large ships could sail as far as Kuntaur, about 48 kilometres (30 miles) past Kau-ur. But nowadays the river is too silted up, as farmers have been clearing the banks for cultivation. So the groundnut mills once situated at Kuntaur have had to be moved downstream to Kau-ur. Here the groundnuts can still be loaded onto ocean-going vessels for export.

Despite this silting up, the river still remains the main artery of the country. Government steamers provide a regular service, for both passengers and cargo, along virtually its whole length, stopping at all the main ports. (Apart from Banjul, these are Kerewan, Balingho, Kau-ur, Kuntaur, Georgetown, Bansang and Basse.) The river does not prove a great barrier between the north and south of the country, either. At least eight public ferries ply between such places as Barra and Banjul. Countless private vessels also use the river constantly, although comparatively few foreign ships are seen, because of the unfortunate political divisions in West Africa.

Nevertheless, there can be little doubt that the River Gambia could be used considerably more. But the Gambian government has always refused to consider making any improvements. The reasons are, of course, mainly political, and stem from the difficulty of making any practical decisions when the river runs through three quite separate and independent countries.

For example, the Gambian government has not been willing

**The Banjul ferry, crowded with people and their belongings**

to do anything about the silting-up of the upper reaches. This is because no dredging operation could possibly be successful without the co-operation of Senegal. Also, a plan for a dam to provide water and electricity for parts of both The Gambia and Senegal has been rejected because the Gambians say it would affect the navigability of their stretch of the river.

The Gambian government has also opposed the building of a bridge across the river. This is partly because the government currently receives large tolls from the ferries. But it is also because a bridge linking, for example, Banjul and Barra would restrict ocean-going ships to the lower reaches of the river, and

46

this would have a serious effect on the country's economy.

It is not only the Gambian government which is opposed to any improvements, however. Most of the farmers whose land lies by the river are afraid of changes of any kind. They rely, for example, on the annual flooding of the river-banks during the rainy season to enable them to grow rice; and they are worried that the construction of a dam would mean the end of their rice crops.

Many of the tourists who visit The Gambia go for a trip along the river. But the river could be of much greater importance to The Gambia than a mere tourist attraction. Hopefully, it will be only a matter of time before The Gambia and Senegal co-operate to make full use of this great waterway, which is a potential source of enormous power, for the benefit of both countries.

# Agriculture

Farming is by far the most important occupation in The Gambia. At least ninety per cent of the country's working population is concerned in some way with agriculture. Farming not only produces the food which the Gambians need themselves, but also provides the country's chief exports, which are its only means (apart from tourism) of obtaining foreign currency.

For centuries the method of farming in The Gambia was what is called "shifting cultivation". This was a system designed to give poor soil a chance to recover after crops had been grown on it. If crops are grown continuously on the same patch of land, the nutrients in the soil are gradually used up and, as a result, harvests diminish. In the past when this happened, the farmers would leave their plots, which were soon covered with bush again, and would not return until they thought the soil had become fertile once more. It was usually about ten years before they went back and cleared the bush away by burning it. Then

48

they dug the ashes into the soil to enrich it, and began farming again. Sometimes whole villages moved, as the farms were transferred from one place to another. This had the advantage that old, insanitary huts were either torn down or abandoned, and the people set up home again in clean, new dwellings.

This system could only work, of course, while the population was small and there was plenty of land available. But in recent years The Gambia's population has increased so rapidly that "shifting cultivation" has almost completely disappeared. The Gambians have had to adjust instead to the idea of just leaving their fields fallow (uncultivated) for a time whenever the soil seemed to be exhausted, and then planting them again with a different type of crop.

By far the most important crop in The Gambia is groundnuts (sometimes called peanuts). They are mostly grown on the upland areas, where the soil is very light. The export of groundnuts provides the government's chief source of revenue, and in recent years nearly 200,000 tonnes have been exported annually.

To grow groundnuts the land is first ploughed, usually with oxen. Then the seeds are sown, generally in June, just before the rainy season starts. Almost every year there are improved varieties of seeds and better fertilizers, but the value of the crop largely depends on whether or not there is exactly the right amount of rain. The crop is harvested in October, before the soil dries out and becomes rock-hard again. It is then sold to the government's marketing board, which fixes the season's

49

**Women at a groundnut-buying station**

price and sends the groundnuts to the factories. In the factories the groundnuts are shelled by modern machinery. Then a large proportion of the crop is pressed, and the valuable groundnut oil extracted. Finally the produce, which includes nuts, oil and cattle-cake (made from what is left when the oil has been extracted), is loaded onto ships to be sent abroad.

Curiously enough, groundnuts did not grow in West Africa until the early nineteenth century. Some people say they were first introduced by slaves who had been set free. The groundnuts certainly came from Brazil, where a great many slaves were taken, and the slaves may well have thought that the groundnuts would provide them with the means of making a living when they returned home.

After groundnuts, the second most important crop in The Gambia is rice. Very little is grown on the uplands, as rice needs swampy conditions during the early life of the plant. The upper river swamps are too narrow and the lower swamps too salty, but the *banto faros* of the middle stretches of the River Gambia are ideal. The rice is usually sown in what can be described as "nursery" paddy-fields. Then, when the seedlings are about 15 centimetres (6 inches) high, they are transplanted into larger flooded fields. It is usually the job of the mother in the family to grow the rice, and she generally surrounds her own piece

**Ploughing a rice field before sowing the rice**

of *banto faros* with an embankment made of a mixture of mud and reeds.

Very little of the rice is sold commercially. Most of it is used to feed the family who have grown it. Nevertheless, rice is the staple diet of virtually all the Gambian people, whether they are able to grow it themselves or not, and so a considerable amount also has to be imported.

On the uplands, where it is too dry for rice, various kinds of millet are grown. The most common type is guinea corn (also sometimes called coos). This is an extremely useful crop, as it not only provides food for the people and their animals, but its tough stems and leaves can also be used for making fences or for hut-building.

**An oil palm plantation**

**A Gambian farmer standing beside his cassava plants. Tapioca is made from cassava**

A small number of oil palms are also grown in The Gambia—mostly in the sandy soil around Banjul. The oil from the fleshy part of the nut is in great demand all over The Gambia for use in cooking. The oil from the kernel, however, is much more difficult to extract; and so the kernels are generally sent to Europe, where the oil is extracted by special machinery and then used in making soap.

The Gambians also grow various minor crops, purely for their own use. These include many of the vegetables grown in Europe, such as turnips, onions, lettuce and tomatoes. But they also grow many tropical vegetables, such as cassava, yams, pumpkins,

53

sweet potatoes and garden egg, as well as such tropical fruit as bananas.

Most of these minor crops are grown by the women of the family. A woman usually has a plot of about half a hectare (1 ¼ acres), roughly half the size of a man's plot. But, whereas the man normally grows crops which he hopes to sell, the woman tries to grow the food she needs to feed her own family.

The rearing of cattle is gradually increasing in importance in The Gambia. Since innoculation against rinderpest (an infectious disease affecting cattle) became compulsory, cattle-rearing has steadily become more and more profitable. Sheep

**Bananas—just one of the tropical fruits grown in The Gambia**

**A small fishing-boat pulling in to the quayside in Banjul**

are also reared, although they are not as important as cattle. Chickens can also be seen in most villages, although they are usually very undersized and lay very small eggs.

Fishing around the coast of The Gambia has not yet been fully exploited. Most of the fishermen refuse to go out of sight of land, because they do not have navigational equipment and are afraid of losing their way. The position is improving, though, as more and more fishermen are managing to buy up-to-date motorized fishing-boats; and small quantities of shrimps and prawns are already being exported to Europe.

## Banjul

The capital of The Gambia is Banjul (formerly called Bathurst). It is situated at the tip of St. Mary's Island, overlooking the River Gambia. The island itself is only about 5 kilometres (3 miles) across, but there is a good road linking it with the rest of the country.

Originally St. Mary's was called Banjola Island. It was first occupied by the British in 1816, as a base from which to intercept any ships carrying slaves. As the river narrows sharply at this point, it was an ideal place to keep a look-out, and many thousands of slaves were freed and sent back to their homes.

Later, Banjul became an important port. A deep channel, which even the largest ships are able to navigate, runs towards Banjul from the open sea. At first, however, ships could not always sail right up to the shore, as the water suddenly becomes shallower close to land; but in 1952 a deep-water quay was constructed, and now all ships can dock easily.

Over half of all The Gambia's exports leave the country

through Banjul. The only other port of any size is Kau-ur, and some of the cargo loaded there is transported as far as Banjul and then transferred onto larger vessels. Groundnuts account for about ninety-three per cent of all exports, with about sixty per cent of these going to Italy and thirty per cent to Britain; and the only other export of any consequence is palm kernels. In addition, almost all the goods imported into The Gambia arrive at Banjul. These mainly consist of cotton goods, rice and machinery of various kinds. About forty per cent of the total imports come from Britain, and the rest are mainly from Japan, India, West Germany and the Netherlands.

As a city, Banjul certainly has a far from ideal location. It is low-lying, swampy and extremely unhealthy. In fact, although a great deal of money has been spent on various drainage schemes, it is still possible to catch fish in the streets in the rainy season! Worse still, the nearby swamps are an ideal breeding-ground for insects—particularly mosquitoes. These have caused a great deal of disease in the past, although modern medicine is at last gaining the upper hand. In addition, the swamps have made it almost impossible for Banjul to expand and, as the population of the city is increasing extremely rapidly, the overcrowding is beginning to reach alarming proportions.

To give an idea of the problem, in 1910 there were only 7,000 people living in Banjul. By 1963 the population had increased to no less than 28,000. Ten years later, the numbers had almost doubled again, and today there may be over 80,000 people, not including numerous temporary residents.

**Workers loading a cargo boat in the port of Banjul**

Over half the population of Banjul are Wolof. These include most of the professional people, such as doctors, dentists, lawyers and teachers. The rest of the professional class is drawn mainly from the Creoles—descendants of slaves who were freed and managed to return to live in Africa. Apart from the Wolof, people from all The Gambia's tribal groups can be found in Banjul. Many of them have settled there only recently, however, in the hope of improving their standard of living. There are also a small number of foreigners who, apart from diplomatic representatives and the like, are nearly all Syrians, and are mostly engaged in some form of trade.

The largest single source of employment in Banjul is naturally the port. In fact, well over half the male population has some connection with the harbour, whether as clerks, dockers or labourers. Most of the other people work as skilled craftsmen (plumbers and carpenters, for example), shop-keepers or domestic workers, or are employed in the public sector by such concerns as the electricity or water boards.

There are very few factories of any kind in Banjul. There is one factory to process groundnuts, similar to the factory at Kau-ur. Apart from this, there are just a few small workshops, making such things as simple articles of furniture or clothing, or cheap souvenirs for the tourists.

The main reason for the lack of industry is the lack of raw materials. The Gambia has no timber, no coal, virtually no minerals and no precious metals, apart from a minute quantity of gold. A very small amount of ilmenite (used in the

**A street scene in Banjul**

**Warehouses near the port in Banjul. The port is Banjul's largest single source of employment**

manufacture of paint) has been found, but the quantity is so small that it has unfortunately not proved economically viable to mine it.

By far the largest area of Banjul is residential. Most of the people still live in small mud huts, built in compounds, as they do in the country districts. But the newer houses are built of wood or stone, and are raised off the ground as a protection against the damp. The shops, offices and schools are scattered in different parts of the city. Unfortunately there is very little space for any kind of outdoor recreation in Banjul, and public parks and gardens are virtually non-existent.

Banjul has no railway station, as there are no trains in The

Gambia. The government has always believed that a railway would take trade away from the river. There is a small international airport, called Yundum, just a short distance from Banjul—but as there are no other airports in The Gambia, there are no internal flights.

Apart from Banjul, the most important town in The Gambia is usually said to be Serekunda. But Serekunda is actually only a small place, about 10 kilometres (7 miles) from the capital. The name is loosely given, however, to a group of five or six small towns, such as Ibo Town and Sara Job Kunda, and together they form a comparatively large urban area.

A town that has recently come to some prominence is Kaur. Since the port of Kuntaur became silted up, many of the boats carrying groundnuts have been loaded up there. Georgetown, on McCarthy Island, has also benefited from the

**A family outside their home in Banjul**

groundnut trade in recent years, as well as from tourists who come to look at its two ruined mud-brick forts.

Another fairly large town is Bansang, which has a hospital built with help from the Save the Children Fund. Other towns include Brikama, Kerewan, Balingho and Basse. Like all the bigger towns in The Gambia, they have only a few stone houses, mostly erected by trading firms or to accommodate government officials; and the rest of the buildings are the usual African huts.

## Family Life

The average visitor to The Gambia sees little more than blue skies and golden sand. Most of the hotels have been built only recently and they are all beside the beaches, well away from any town. The food and drink are as much as possible like those the tourists are used to, and the tour companies try to ensure that the service is up to European standards.

For the Gambians themselves life is very different. Only a very small number live in the way any European would consider pleasant or comfortable. In fact, the majority of them still live in almost exactly the same way as their parents and grandparents did, fifty or even a hundred years ago.

The average Gambian home is a mud hut with a straw roof. The roof usually stretches out a metre (3 feet) or so beyond the walls, to protect the mud walls from the rain. This means there is a kind of verandah, where people often store their possessions, such as jars of grain. They sometimes stretch a piece of matting out there, too, so that they can sit in the shade.

**Traditional mud huts with straw roofs**

The walls inside the hut are made of basket-work. On these, the Gambians usually hang clay pots, baskets of seeds, and perhaps their hoes and axes. The floor is made of beaten earth, and has usually had palm kernels set into it while the earth was still wet, to give it a firm, hard surface. It is generally covered with mats made of sisal or with coconut matting. There is often no light in the hut, not even a candle. But a fire is normally kept smouldering, to keep away the mosquitoes. This means the inside of the hut is always very dark and smoky, but the Gambians do not seem to mind, because at least they are protected from the fierce rays of the sun.

Most Gambian families have one, or even two other huts in

64

which they sleep. So, in effect, a hut is not a whole house, but merely the equivalent of one room of a house. Nevertheless, the huts must seem extremely cramped—especially in the rainy season, when it is too wet to do the cooking or to have meals out of doors, as the Gambians usually do during the rest of the year.

The poorest huts are generally the ones just beside the river. These are usually just temporary dwellings, which the people put up while they are working on the *banto faros* and later pull down or abandon. On the other hand, the more prosperous villages have huts which are built from sun-dried bricks made out of clay and straw. These huts are laid out beside straight roads, and look quite substantial.

The Gambians normally live in what is called an "extended family". This means that everyone in the village is related to everyone else. These ties of kinship are very strong, and a Gambian would not think of living in any other village, because that would mean leaving his relatives and living among strangers. As a result all the villagers think it is quite natural to help each other. For example, when the adults go to work the babies are left with any other adult or older child who does not happen to be working. But by the time the children are about seven years old they are usually considered old enough to help the adults in the fields themselves.

People usually work, with only a snack for lunch, until nearly sunset. Then they have their main meal of the day, which consists largely of rice. There is generally a good selection of

65

vegetables, however, which the family have grown themselves, as well as cheese of some kind, various nuts and sometimes eggs. There may also be fish, as these abound in the River Gambia. They are caught in funnel-shaped traps made of reeds, which are placed in the water in the evening. However, there is very rarely any meat, or even chicken, except on some special feast day. Cattle and sheep are kept mainly for their milk, and chickens are usually kept only for their eggs.

In the evening the villagers sometimes light a big bonfire. Then the men get out their drums, and everyone sings and dances. The children are always there as well, as no one ever thinks of putting them to bed early. They either join in the singing and dancing or just amuse themselves together.

One way the children often amuse themselves is by making tops out of gourds with sticks stuck through them. They also play skittles with pieces of wood stood on end, and some hard fruit as balls. The boys have blow-pipes, which they make for themselves out of hollow reeds, and the girls have dolls, which are generally made out of clay. One of the most popular games is rather like marbles. The children make a hole in the ground which they line with banana leaves, and then they roll groundnuts around in the hole. They also play board games, and one of the most common is a version of draughts, played with two sets of stones, one black and one white, on a board scratched on the ground.

Disease is still a great source of misery for most families in The Gambia. Almost all the well-known tropical diseases are

**Gambian children on the road leading to their village**

still to be found throughout the country. There are three main reasons for this. One is the presence of disease-carrying insects, particularly mosquitoes, another is poor sanitation, and the third is malnutrition, arising mainly from the lack of protein and vitamins in the diet.

By far the commonest disease in The Gambia is malaria. This is transmitted mainly by mosquitoes, and kills many babies. Almost everyone in The Gambia has had malaria at some time

**A man suffering from river blindness being led across a Banjul street**

or other, and some people have recurring attacks, leaving them physically weak and often mentally affected, as well.

Another very common disease is bilharzia. This affects people who work in the *banto faros*, or elsewhere near the river, and is particularly difficult to treat. It is caused by a tiny parasite which lives in the water. Once this parasite gets under the skin of a sufferer, he quickly becomes extremely weak. Even if the patient is cured by modern drugs, the moment he goes back to work and stands with bare feet in the muddy water he is likely to contract the disease again.

Apart from malaria and bilharzia, other common diseases in The Gambia are meningitis, which causes thousands of deaths every year, leprosy, yellow fever, tuberculosis and cholera.

68

# Sport and Entertainment

The traditional sport for boys and men in The Gambia is wrestling. This has been popular at least since the early days of the Mali Empire. The winners of wrestling matches at that period were regarded as national heroes, and were only a little below the tribal leaders themselves in public esteem.

Wrestling tournaments are held at Brikama and Serekunda almost every week, but in recent years these have tended to be mainly spectacles to entertain the tourists. The more traditional wrestling matches arc held in makeshift rings in the villages, with small crowds of supporters sitting around on tree stumps or on the ground.

Officially, wrestlers are divided into three classes—heavy, middle and light weight. But in fact the wrestlers are usually willing to fight almost anyone, as long as he belongs to their own tribe. Punching, kicking, biting and even throwing sand are not necessarily considered the best way of winning, but they are quite often overlooked by the referee! The scoring is simple, with the first man down being the loser. The winner then goes on to fight the next challenger, and so on. Between the bouts there is generally some loud flute-playing, or the raucous singing of tribal songs, while one of the seconds goes round with the hat among the crowd.

In recent years, however, football has begun to replace wrestling. Young Gambians play it barefoot on the beach or on any other rough piece of ground they can find. There is only one place in The Gambia where there are professional matches, though, and that is the Box Bar Stadium in Banjul, which is nearly always crowded with fans at the weekends.

Other Western sports have little or no following in The Gambia. The average young Gambian has no money to buy either expensive sports equipment or special clothes. There is a tennis and basket-ball club in Banjul, but it is frequented mainly by foreigners; and most of the swimming-pools are in the grounds of the hotels.

Like nearly all Africans, the Gambians are fond of music. Almost every family has a few primitive instruments, which they like to bring out and play in the evenings.

The most important instruments in Gambian music are the drums. These vary from the very high-pitched drums used by the Wolof to the extremely deep ones used by the Mandingo. There are also long conical drums, barrel-shaped drums, kettle-drums and a curious kind of drum played in sets of four, which all produce their own distinctive sound. In the past these drums were used to send messages from one village to another. They were also beaten on special occasions, such as when a chief was elected or when he died. Most of the drums can only be beaten for an hour or so, however, because after that the skins begin to sag, and the drums begin to lose their correct tone.

Apart from drums, one of the most popular instruments is the *kora*. This is mainly used by the Mandingo, although other tribes sometimes play rather similar instruments. The *kora* is a kind of harp, with twenty-one strings arranged in two staves, and it is played almost entirely with the thumbs, without any help from the fingers.

Another popular instrument is known as the *keno*. It is only

**Dancing to the rhythm of the drums in a small Gambian village**

played by the Mandingo and the Fula, but again other tribes have rather similar instruments. The *keno* is something like a small banjo. Its body is made of a gourd tightly covered with cow-hide, which still has the animal's hair attached to it.

Several tribes also play lutes, which usually have five strings. These can either be plucked or strummed, and are often played at Muslim religious festivals. There are also one-stringed fiddles, which are mainly played by the Wolof and the Fula. These usually have their string made out of a thin twisted piece of cow-hide or antelope-hide.

Most Gambians are good at singing. They learn to sing either at home or at school, and usually harmonize simply but well. There are several excellent Christian choirs, including one attached to the Catholic Cathedral in Banjul, which was founded in 1976 and is known as the "Baati Linguere" or "Pure Voice" Choir.

The Gambians, like all Africans, also enjoy dancing. In the villages the dances are naturally very simple, and everyone joins in the fun. However, in 1975 the Gambian National Troupe of Dancers was formed. This performs mainly for tourists, and has reached a very high level of accomplishment. The Troupe consists of both men and women and has about a dozen members. They always dance barefoot, and nearly always in the open air. They have a variety of costumes, but the women usually wear a skirt reaching just below the knees and a gaily coloured bandeau top, while the men usually also wear skirts and feathered head-dresses. Many of the dances performed by the Troupe originated many centuries ago. One dance represents the celebrations held after the harvest has been gathered in. Another is an exciting masked dance, in which the dancers represent either good or evil, and each group tries to cast magic spells upon the other.

The Fula are also well-known for their acrobatics. A group of them regularly perform in the hotels around Banjul to entertain the tourists. Some of the Fula also present a fire-eating act, with bundles of burning grass, accompanied by the usual beating of gourd drums and perhaps a fiddle or a flute.

# Education

One of the most familiar sounds in The Gambia used to be a high-pitched chanting. This told everyone within earshot that children were attending a Quranic school. Each school belonged to a mosque, but the two buildings were not always together. The school might have been quite a distance away, in a private house, a hut or a room behind a shop.

The children who attended these schools were all boys, aged between five and twelve. They sat cross-legged in a circle round their teacher, who held a long stick in one hand. The boys had no books, but they usually balanced a small board on their knees, and copied on the boards with a reed pen dipped in thin ink made from burnt wool and water.

The method of teaching was practically always the same. The teacher read a verse from the *Quran*, and the boys repeated it over and over again, swaying backwards and forwards. Then the boys wrote down on their boards the verses they had been repeating, and any boy who had not learnt them all by heart at the end of the day was very likely to get a harsh beating.

Occasionally a little reading and writing and some simple arithmetic were also taught. But how much the boys learnt depended chiefly on how much the master himself happened to know! The boys usually went to school for a few hours every day, except on Friday, and on the last day of the week they would give the teacher a small payment, in money or in kind.

Today these old Quranic schools have virtually disappeared

**A Quranic teacher with two of his students**

in The Gambia. But in 1978 the Gambian government passed a law that Quranic studies must be taught in all the state schools in future. This has meant a return to almost exactly the same methods of teaching as before, with the boys repeating verse after verse of the *Quran*, at least once a day, and sometimes twice.

Education is not yet compulsory in The Gambia, but the government is doing its best to ensure that as many children as possible go to school. Children start school at eight years of age, and it is hoped that they will stay until they have completed the primary stage of education, when they are fourteen years old.

This may not seem a very ambitious plan of education. But it should be remembered that when the British ruled The Gambia not more than twenty per cent of the children went to school at all. Now the hope is that all the children in The Gambia will eventually go to school for at least seven years, once more schools have been built and a sufficient number of teachers trained.

Many Gambians cannot see the need to send their children to school, however. They think they can get on quite well as farmers and herdsmen even if they cannot read or write. In any case, there is very little to read in The Gambia, as there are very few books to be bought or borrowed, and only one newspaper, which appears three times a week. The Gambians are often particularly reluctant to allow girls to be educated. They think that a girl will learn much more by just watching her mother than she ever will at school. Added to this, girls are often a great help in the home, looking after the babies while

76

**A small primary school. The Gambian government hopes that eventually all children will go to school for at least seven years**

the parents are out at work, and the parents are usually very reluctant to lose their assistance.

At the last census (in 1980), the total number of children at school was 43,000. But some of them (particularly the girls) only attended rather irregularly. About 35,000 children were attending primary schools and the rest were in the secondary schools. There were 25 secondary schools, nearly all in the Banjul area, and 133 primary schools.

When children first go to school in The Gambia, they are taught in their own local language. But, in the secondary schools, they are usually all taught in Mandingo—unless they live in Banjul, where they are taught in Wolof. Unfortunately, there are very few text-books available in any of the African languages

**Goods being delivered to a professional letter-writer in Banjul. Although the government is keen to improve education, many people are still unable to read or write**

at the moment, and this tends to slow down the children's progress considerably. In a few of the secondary schools, however, nearly all the lessons are conducted in English. These are the schools which aim to send the children on to some kind of higher education. The best known is probably the Gambian High School in Banjul, but there are two similar schools run by the Gambian Muslim Association, and one run by the Roman Catholic Mission.

There are only three colleges of higher education in The Gambia. The largest is the Brikama College (formerly known as the Yundum College). Students at Brikama College can study

78

agriculture, domestic science, rural studies and health education, and there is also a department devoted to teacher training.

If Gambian students want to go to university they must go abroad. Most of them go to Sierra Leone, as this is the nearest English-speaking country in Africa, but some go to Britain or the United States. They can only go abroad if their parents are wealthy, as there is little or no government aid available.

A few Gambians also go to the Al-Azhar University, in Cairo, in Egypt. This was founded in A.D. 972, and is considered the "Mother University" of the whole Muslim world. The students there receive their education entirely free, and if they are poor they are even provided with accommodation and food. They do, however, have to pay their own fare to Cairo.

As well as the normal school holidays, Gambian children have numerous public holidays. These include certain Muslim feast-days, such as the birth of Muhammad (December 17th) and the last day of Ramadan. But they also include many Christian feasts, such as Christmas, Easter and the Assumption, as well as political holidays like Independence Day (February 18th) and Labour Day (May 1st).

Children who do not attend school may learn a little by listening to the radio. (There is no television service in The Gambia at the moment.) There is a government broadcasting station, which is on the air for twelve hours a day, and a commercial station, called Radio Syd, which is on the air for fifteen hours, but neither of these stations broadcast many programmes which are specifically designed to be educational.

# The Gambia and Senegal

The Republic of Senegal is the only country that has a common border with The Gambia. In fact, apart from the short stretch of land facing the Atlantic, the whole of The Gambia is surrounded by Senegal. What is more, the River Gambia flows through Senegal before entering The Gambia; and so the two countries have a direct link in the waterway which is so vital to The Gambia's very existence.

The history of Senegal is also very closely interwoven with that of The Gambia. Both formed part of the extensive Mali Empire and, for nearly twenty years in the eighteenth century, were actually joined together to form the country of Senegambia. Moreover, as we shall see, several tribal groups are common to both countries. It is, therefore, very difficult to consider one country in isolation from the other, and we shall now look briefly at Senegal to see how it compares with The Gambia.

Unlike The Gambia, Senegal has several important waterways. The largest of these is the River Senegal in the extreme north of the country. This bursts its banks every year, making the land beside it very fertile. The chief crops in this flood area are groundnuts and millet, but a large-scale irrigation scheme has recently been carried out near the delta so that rice can be grown there as well. Another very important product in this area is gum arabic, which comes from the acacia tree. At one time this was by far the most valuable cash crop in Senegal. Even today, thousands of tonnes are exported annually, to be used in pharmacy, in cooking and for various processes in the textile trade.

To the south and east of this fertile area is the Ferlo desert. This is so large that it takes up well over one-third of the whole country. It is not true desert, as it is a mixture of low sand-dunes and clay depressions, but very little will grow there, and it is mostly uninhabited.

Between the Ferlo desert and the sea is the Cayor region. This has dunes, but it also has many marshy depressions which make quite good farm-land. In addition, it has much more rain than the Ferlo desert, and oil palms, bananas, coconuts and all kinds of vegetables can be grown there successfully.

The remainder of Senegal lies around the Gambian enclave. To the north and south the soil is reasonably fertile and, as in The Gambia, the chief crop is groundnuts. To the east, however, there are sandy uplands, where very little will grow, and the country is almost as uninhabited as is the Ferlo desert.

The capital of Senegal is the great port of Dakar, situated on the tip of the Cape Verde peninsula, in the north of the

**The great port of Dakar, in the north of Senegal**

country. Dakar has a population of well over half a million (approximately six or seven times the size of Banjul), and is generally considered to be the most westernized city in West Africa.

The next most important city is Saint-Louis, at the mouth of the River Senegal. This was founded by the French in 1633, and was at one time the capital of the country. The other large cities, such as Thies, Rufisque and Kaolack, all owe their foundation to being collecting or distributing points for the groundnut trade, as they still are today.

The government is worried, however, by the growth of large cities, like Dakar. People are leaving the country areas and

82

flooding in there at the rate of more than six per cent per year. In fact, two-thirds of the entire population now live in only one quarter of the country—roughly the area that runs along by the Atlantic—and the rest of the country is becoming seriously short of inhabitants.

There are at least six quite distinct ethnic groups in Senegal. Some of them, such as the Wolof, are also found in The Gambia. The reason for this is that the white settlers took no account at all of tribal boundaries when they decided on the frontiers for their new colonies, and even tiny villages found themselves partly in one country and partly in another.

The Wolof are by far the largest group in Senegal. They represent about one-third of the total population, and predominate in the west of the country. Although some of the Wolof live in cities, they are primarily groundnut farmers, living

**A street in Saint Louis, former capital of Senegal**

in small nomadic groups of about one hundred families and moving from place to place as the soil becomes exhausted.

The next largest group are the Serere. They also live in the west of the country, but mostly between The Gambia and the Cayor region of Senegal. They probably number about three-quarters of a million, and are generally nomadic farmers, growing yams, maize and millet as well as groundnuts.

The Fula are to be found in almost every part of Senegal. They, too, are farmers, but they usually live in permanent, settled villages. The smaller ethnic groups include the Tukulor (who are often hard to distinguish from the Wolof), the Dyola and (in the south) the Mandingo.

Politically Senegal is a parliamentary democracy. It has a president, a prime minister and a national assembly which is elected by popular vote. Officially there can be any number of different political parties, but in fact there is only one of any size, although there are various divisions of different kinds within the party.

Senegal is proud of the fact that its regime is liberal. It believes that Senegal should be a land for black people, in which all black people have equal rights and responsibilities. In fact, it can be described as a socialist country, in which the government tries to impose controls by persuasion rather than in an authoritarian manner. There is no nationalization, except for the marketing of groundnuts and other agricultural products. Private investors, both Senegalese and foreign, are encouraged. Not surprisingly, most of the foreigners are French, as Senegal has French as its

**A Fula wedding. The Fula are just one of the ethnic groups common to both The Gambia and Senegal**

official language, and uses the franc as the basis for all its commercial dealings.

Although Senegal and The Gambia have had their differences of opinion in the past, in the last few years they have been increasingly working together to help their respective economies. In 1982, the Senegambian Confederation came into existence. Although each country retains the right to govern itself, the confederation enables them to work together in many areas for their mutual benefit. Each country will still have its own parliament for internal government, but it is planned that there will be a joint parliament and a joint foreign policy (although each country will retain its own diplomatic missions abroad). A monetary union is also planned, which means that both countries will have the same coinage (at present, The Gambia uses the *dalasi*, which is divided into one hundred *butus*, while the Senegalese unit of currency is the franc). A customs union will bring The Gambia's low tariffs into line with the higher tariffs of Senegal. There will be an integrated health service. The Gambia (which has no military forces of any kind) will be protected by Senegal's forces, and there may eventually even be a bi-lingual Civil Service to run the affairs of the two countries.

# The Gambia in the Modern World

If a Gambian were asked his nationality, he might well say he was a Mandingo or a Fula. For many Gambians, their tribe is still much more important to them than their country. In fact, many Gambians feel much closer to people in other parts of West Africa, who belong to the same tribe and speak the same language, than they do to members of other tribal groups within The Gambia itself.

It may seem rather strange that members of one tribe can live in different countries. It was the European settlers, not the Africans themselves, who were responsible for this. In most cases, each European nation just claimed a large area of territory with no regard at all for the ancient tribal boundaries. Similarly, each nation imposed its own language and system of government on the land it claimed, with the result that there are now countless artificial barriers between the different countries which make up modern West Africa and even within individual countries.

This lack of unity is, unfortunately, a considerable stumbling-block to The Gambia's development. If it is to progress at all in the modern world, its people must be united and realize that they must all work together for the common good.

Another problem is The Gambia's small size—it is barely as big as one of the larger English counties and certainly smaller than most American states, with an area of just over 10,000 square kilometres (4,000 square miles).

The Gambia is not only small, it is also a very poor country. In comparison with the rest of West Africa, its natural resources are extremely meagre. Most of West Africa is very rich in minerals of one kind or another (indeed, this was the main attraction for most of the European settlers), and today minerals are high on the list of foreign currency-earners for most countries in the region. Mauritania, Mali, Liberia and Sierra Leone all export iron ore, Togo exports copper and phosphates and Nigeria exports tin. The Congo and Nigeria both export crude petroleum, and a number of other countries, particularly south of Senegal, export bauxite, from which aluminium is produced. The Gambia, however, has no mineral deposits of any consequence.

Moreover, there is only one crop that can be exported in any great quantity, and that is groundnuts. But, as we have seen, groundnuts grow particularly well in the savannah or grasslands—and the savannah covers an extremely large area of West Africa. It covers practically the whole of The Gambia and Senegal, apart from the area beside the River Gambia and

88

**A public tap by a typical house in Banjul — an example of The Gambia's poverty and lack of raw materials**

the coastal areas. And it also covers the south of Mali and the greater part of Nigeria. Groundnuts are the principal crop throughout this region and, in fact, Nigeria is easily the largest exporter of groundnuts in the world. This means, of course, that The Gambia is unable to trade to any appreciable extent with the rest of West Africa. If The Gambia wishes to export its groundnuts, it has no choice but to send them to Europe; and the few goods it imports (mainly cars and machinery) usually come from the European countries as well.

**Sacks of groundnuts awaiting shipment**

The Gambia's only other means of earning foreign currency is by attracting tourists. The tourist trade has increased rapidly in recent years, but whether this rapid expansion will continue is rather doubtful. The Gambia is too far from Europe to rival Spain, for example, in beach holidays; and it has little else to offer holiday-makers apart from bird-watching and visits to the nature reserve at Abuko, just a short distance from Banjul.

Apart from the links it is now forging with Senegal, The Gambia plays little part in West African affairs. This is largely because it is the only English-speaking nation in this part of West Africa. Its nearest English-speaking neighbour is Sierra Leone, nearly 500 kilometres (300 miles) to the south. Similarly, The Gambia is isolated from all the other Commonwealth countries. Its nearest Commonwealth neighbour is again Sierra

Leone. This is, of course, yet another legacy from the days when the European nations divided up West Africa between themselves, without any regard for the people who lived there.

The Gambia is naturally represented at Commonwealth conferences and at the United Nations but, being so small, it takes very little active part in world affairs. It has no army, navy or air-force, and its entire annual economic turnover is barely as great as that of a comparatively small European city.

One final example will perhaps show how isolated The Gambia is from even its most immediate neighbours—the railway in Senegal is forced to make a long, tortuous detour to ensure that it does not cross the border into The Gambia. Perhaps when The Gambia forms some kind of federation with Senegal, the situation will improve and at least some measure of prosperity will come to this tiny African nation.

# Index